Piece *of* Pi

Wit-Sharpening, Brain-Bruising, Number-Crunching Activities With Pi

Written by **Naila Bokhari**   Illustrated by **S. O'Shaughnessy**

Published by Prufrock Press Inc.

Copyright ©2008 Prufrock Press Inc.

Printed in the United States of America.

ISBN-13: 978-1-59363-120-8
ISBN-10: 1-59363-120-0

Prufrock Press, Inc.
P.O. Box 8813
Waco, Texas 76714-8813
(800) 998-2208
Fax (800) 240-0333
http://www.prufrock.com

Contents

Introduction · 5

Information for the Instructor · · · · · · · · · · · · · 6

   Interesting Pi Facts · · · · · · · · · · · · · · · · · · 7

   A Chronology of Pi · · · · · · · · · · · · · · · · · 8

Lessons for Exploring Pi

   Discovering Pi · 11

   Aryabhata's Value For Π · · · · · · · · · · · · · · 14

   Pi and the Bible · · · · · · · · · · · · · · · · · · 16

   Srinavasa Ramanujan (the Geometric Method) · · · · · · 18

   Circular Pi · 21

   Estimations and Computations For Pi · · · · · · · · · 23

   Hats Off to Pi · · · · · · · · · · · · · · · · · · · 25

   Pi and the Greek Alphabet · · · · · · · · · · · · · 27

   Buffon's Needle Experiment · · · · · · · · · · · · · 29

   Finding the Square Root of Pi · · · · · · · · · · · · 31

   Using Random Numbers · · · · · · · · · · · · · · · 33

   Archimedes' Method · · · · · · · · · · · · · · · · · 36

Extra Activities and Material

   Where Do You Find Pi? · · · · · · · · · · · · · · · 40

   Remembering Pi · · · · · · · · · · · · · · · · · · · 41

   Glossary · 42

   Information About Mathematicians · · · · · · · · · · 43

   Resources for Pi · · · · · · · · · · · · · · · · · · 48

Common Core State Standards Alignment Sheet
Piece of Pi

All lessons in this book align to the following standards.

Grade Level	Common Core State Standards in Math
Grade 5	5.OA.A Write and interpret numerical expressions. 5.OA.B Analyze patterns and relationships. 5.NBT.A Understand the place value system. 5.NF.A Use equivalent fractions as a strategy to add and subtract fractions. 5.NF.B Apply and extend previous understandings of multiplication and division. 5.MD.A Convert like measurement units within a given measurement system. 5.MD.C Geometric measurement: understand concepts of volume. 5.G.A Graph points on the coordinate plane to solve real-world and mathematical problems.
Grade 6	6.RP.A Understand ratio concepts and use ratio reasoning to solve problems. 6.NS.C Apply and extend previous understandings of numbers to the system of rational numbers. 6.EE.A Apply and extend previous understandings of arithmetic to algebraic expressions. 6.EE.B Reason about and solve one-variable equations and inequalities.
Grade 7	7.RP.A Analyze proportional relationships and use them to solve real-world and mathematical problems. 7.G.A Draw construct, and describe geometrical figures and describe the relationships between them. 7.G.B Solve real-life and mathematical problems involving angle measure, area, surface area, and volume. 7.SP.A Use random sampling to draw inferences about a population. 7.SP.C Investigate chance processes and develop, use, and evaluate probability models.
Grade 8	8.NS.A Know that there are numbers that are not rational, and approximate them by rational numbers. 8.EE.A Expressions and Equations Work with radicals and integer exponents. 8.G.C Solve real-world and mathematical problems involving volume of cylinders, cones, and spheres. 8.G.B Understand and apply the Pythagorean Theorem.
High School	HSG-CO.D Make geometric constructions.

Key:

OA = Operations & Algebraic Thinking; NBT = Number & Operations in Base Ten; NF = Number & Operations–Fractions; MD = Measurement & Data; G = Geometry; RP = Ratios & Proportional Relationships; NS = The Number System; EE = Expressions and Equations; SP = Statistics & Probability; HSG-CO = High School Geometry–Congruence

Introduction

There are some topics or problems in mathematics that have captured the interest of mathematicians for ages. Calculating pi is one of them. Thousands of years ago people realized that there was a consistent relationship between a circle's diameter and circumference. Over time, mathematicians have been able to approximate a value for pi with greater and greater accuracy. Doing this has involved a variety of methods, including probability, random numbers, geometry, square root and calculus. In addition to this quest for an accurate approximation, scholars have discovered many interesting, related subjects. What has intrigued mathematicians for ages is readily available to your students with the guided activities in *A Piece of Pi*.

Why Pi?

This marvelous infinite number we know as pi shows up in many fascinating and mysterious ways. It can be found everywhere, from astronomy and probability to the physics of sound and light. It is one of the most important numbers that exists.

Students often encounter pi in the mathematics classroom when applying various formulas, but rarely do they use or explore pi in other creative contexts. The NCTM standards call for a depth of learning, connections to other disciplines and students' engagement in their own learning process. *A Piece of Pi* addresses these specific areas as well as a continuum of other national standards. It focuses on step-by-step exploration and higher-level thinking activities involving pi, many with a multicultural emphasis.

Pi Day

These investigations can be culminated with a celebration on 'Pi Day.' Pi Day is March 14th beginning at 1:59 p.m. (3/14 at 1:59, which when written as a decimal is the number that approximates pi, 3.14159). Presentation of activities outlined in this book encourages active engagement of students' creative process as they present their knowledge of this infinite, irrational number. In addition to the calculations and experiments presented in this text, students can stage skits showing the history of pi, write pi poetry, find fascinating pi facts, make displays that show where pi is used, and have a quiz-bowl-type competition on events, people and calculations related to pi.

Although it is an unofficial celebration, I have celebrated Pi Day with my junior high students. Every year, on March 14th, at exactly 1:59 p.m. (3.14159) students demonstrate their knowledge of the infinite number through presentations to the whole school. This activity, which taps into various intelligences, fosters creativity and enjoyment of mathematics and leaves a lasting effect on the students and the audience. Once the presentations are over, all students indulge in homemade pies.

Bringing Pi to Life

Breathing life into mathematics gives purpose and meaning to what students are learning. *A Piece of Pi* is a way to help students recreate the experiments and calculations that have helped people expand their understanding of pi from a number that was "about 3" to an infinite number that has been calculated to over 51 billion decimal places. Using all or part of the activities in this book will bring the essence of being a mathematician to life in your classroom.

Information for the Instructor

Lesson Organization

This book contains a collection of interesting information, famous pi quotes, a chronology of pi and reproducible classroom activities. All activities are in line with the NCTM standards and can be used to complement any mathematics program in fifth grade through eighth grade. The classroom activities can be adapted to all ability and grade levels.

Each complete lesson plan includes:
- Learning objectives
- NCTM standards
- Suggested grade levels
- Time frame
- Recommended group size
- Materials required
- Prerequisites
- Procedure
- Reproducible sheets necessary for the activity
- Extension activities

What Is Pi?

Pi is both the sixteenth letter of the Greek alphabet and the symbol that represents the world's oldest mathematical mystery: the ratio of a circle's circumference to its diameter. Pi is a number, a universal constant that can be found everywhere, from astronomy to probability to the physics of sound and light. It is one of the most important numbers that exists. The numbers that are most often associated with pi (3¹⁄₇, 3.14, and 3.1416) are rational approximations to pi, which is a non-repeating irrational decimal.

From very early times, people have attempted to estimate the value of pi. The Babylonians, Indians, and Chinese used a value of 3 as a general estimate of pi. Pi possibly entered human consciousness in Egypt. The earliest known written record of the ratio comes from a middle Kingdom papyrus scroll, written around 1650 B.C. by a scribe named Ahmes. He calculated the value to be 3.16 (a mere 1% off the true value). Although we have methods to calculate the digits of pi, its exact value remains a mystery.

It wasn't until 1761 that Johann Heinrich Lambert showed that pi was irrational. Since 1794, when it was proven that pi was both irrational and infinite, people have been searching for a pattern in the endless string of numbers.

Physicists have noted the ubiquity of pi in nature. Pi is obvious in the disks of the moon and the sun. The double helix of DNA revolves around pi. Pi hides in the rainbow, and sits in the pupil of the eye, and when a raindrop falls into water, pi emerges in the spreading rings. Pi can be found in waves and ripples and spectra of all kinds, and therefore pi occurs in colors and music. Pi has lately turned up in superstrings.

Pi occurs naturally in tables of death, in what is known as a Gaussian distribution of deaths in a population. It is found in sine waves and navigation. It truly is one of the great mysteries why nature seems to know mathematics.

In the words of William L. Schaaf in *Nature and History of π*:

> *"Probably no symbol in mathematics has evoked as much mystery, romanticism, misconception and human interest as the number pi (π)."*

Interesting Pi Facts

1. Albert Einstein was born on Pi Day (3/14/1879).

2. Pi is the name of the East German spy organization in Alfred Hitchcock's 1966 film *Torn Curtain*.

3. The Great Pyramid at Giza has a fascinating relationship inherent in its structure. The ratio of the length of one side to the height is approximately $\pi/2$.

4. In order to obtain 100 digits of pi using the Gregory-Leibniz series, you would have to calculate more terms than there are particles in the universe.

5. If a string were tied around the equator of the earth (assuming that the earth were perfectly round), the string would have to be 2π feet longer in order to sit 1 foot off the surface of the globe.

6. There are no occurrences of the sequence 123456 in the first million digits of pi. But of the eight 12345s, three are followed by another 5. The sequence 012345 occurs twice, and in both cases it is followed by another 5.

7. The three numbers 3, 31, and 314,159 are prime. If you reverse the order of these, you also get other prime numbers: 951,413, 13 and 3.

8. If a billion digits of pi were printed in ordinary type, it would extend over 1,200 miles.

9. In the Star Trek episode "Wolf in the Fold," Spock fools the evil computer by telling it to "compute to the last digit the value of pi."

10. The sequence 123456789 first appears at the 523,551,502nd digit.

11. The height of an elephant (from foot to shoulder) = $2 \cdot \pi \cdot$ the diameter of its foot.

12. If you take 10 million random digits, statistically on average you would expect 200 cases where you get 5 digits in a row the same. If you take 10 million digits of pi, you get exactly 200 occurrences.

13. If a billion decimals of pi were printed in ordinary type, they would stretch from New York City to the middle of Kansas.

14. For the circumference of a circle to equal pi the diameter must be 1.

15. At position 763 there are six nines in a row. This is known as the Feynman Point.

16. In ancient Greece the symbol for pi (Π) denoted the number 80.

Chronology of Pi

c. 2000 B.C.   Babylonians use $\pi = \frac{25}{8} = 3.125$

                               Egyptians use $\pi = \frac{256}{81} = 3.1605$

c. 1100 B.C.   Chinese use $\pi = 3$

c. 900 B.C.   *Bible*, I Kings 7:23 implies $\pi = 3$

c. 434 B.C.   Anaxagoras attempts to square the circle

c. 430 B.C.   Antiphon and Bryson articulate the principle of exhaustion.

c. 414 B.C.   Aristophanes refers to squaring the circle in his comedy *The Birds*.

c. 335 B.C.   Dinstratos uses the quadratrix to "square the circle."

c. 240 B.C.   Archimedes uses a 96-sided polygon to show that $\frac{223}{71} < \pi < \frac{22}{7}$. He also uses a spiral to square the circle.

second century A.D.   Claudius Ptolemy uses $\pi = 3° \, 8' \, 30'' = \frac{377}{120} = 3.14166$.

third century A.D.   Wang Fau uses $\pi = \frac{142}{45} = 3.1555$

263 A.D.   Liu Hui uses $\pi = \frac{157}{50} = 3.14$.

c. 480   Tsu Ch'ung-chih approximates π by $\frac{355}{113} = 3.1415929203$ using a circle 10 feet across

c. 530   Aryabhata uses $\pi = 62{,}832/20{,}000 = 3.1416$.

c. 650   Brahmagupta uses $\pi = \sqrt{10} = 3.162$

1220   Leonardo de Pisa (Fibonacci) finds $\pi = 3.141818$.

1429   Al-Kashi calculates π to 16 decimal places.

1593   Francois Viete expresses π as an infinite product using only 2s and πs. Adriaen Romanus finds pi to 15 decimal places.

1610   Ludolph van Ceulen calculates pi to 35 places.

1621   Willebrod Snell refines Archimedes' classical method.

1630   Grienberger uses Snell's refinement to calculate π to 39 decimal places.

1654   Huygens proves the validity of Snell's refinement.

1655	John Wallis finds an infinite rational product for pi. Brouncker converts it to a continued fraction.
1663	Muramatsu Shigekiyo finds seven accurate digits in Japan.
1665-66	Isaac Newton discovers calculus and calculates pi to at least 16 decimal places. This was not published until 1737.
1671	James Gregory discovers the arctangent series.
1674	Gottfried Wilhelm Leibniz discovers the arctangent series for pi: $\pi/4 = 1 - \frac{1}{3} + \frac{1}{5} - \frac{1}{7} + \ldots$
1699	Abraham Sharp uses Gregory's series with $x = \sqrt{3}$ to calculate π to 71 decimal places.
1706	John Machin calculate pi to 100 places. William Jones uses the symbol π to describe the ratio between the circumference of a circle and its diameter.
1713	Chinese court publishes *Su-li Ching-yun*, which shows pi to 19 digits.
1717	Abraham Sharp finds the value of pi to 72 places.
1719	Thomas Fantet de Lagny calculates pi to 127 places.
1722	Takebe Kenko finds 40 digits in Japan.
1736	Leonhard Euler proves that $1/1^2 + \frac{1}{2}^2 + 1/3^2 + \ldots = \pi^2/6$.
1737	Euler uses the symbol π, thus establishing it as standard notation.
1755	Euler derives a very rapidly converging arctangent series.
1761	Johann Heinrich Lambert shows that pi is irrational.
1767	Johann Lambert proves that pi is an irrational number, that is, it has no pattern and cannot be exactly equal to the ratio of two natural numbers.
1775	Euler suggests that pi is transcendental.
1777	Comte de Buffon devises his needle problem.
1794	George Vega calculates pi to 140 decimal places. A.M. Legendre proves the irrationality of π and π^2.
1844	Johann Dase and L.K. Schulz von Stassnitzky calculate pi to 200 places in under two months.
1855	Richter calculates pi to 500 decimal places.

1873	Charles Hermite proves the transcendence of pi.
1873-74	William Shanks calculates pi to 707 decimal places.
1874	Seng Chi-Hung finds 100 digits in China.
1882	Ferdinand von Lindermann shows that pi is transcendental, so the circle cannot be squared.
1945	D. F. Ferguson finds errors, starting with the 528th place in Shanks' value for pi.
1948	Ferguson and Wrench publish corrected value of pi to 808 decimal places, a feat that took about one year.
1949	ENIAC performs first electronic computation of pi to 2,037 decimal places in seventy hours.
1955	NORC computes 3,089 decimals in thirteen minutes.
1959	IBM 704 (Paris) computes 16,167 decimal places.
1961	Daniel Shanks and John Wrench use IBM 7090 (New York) to compute 100,200 decimal places in 8.72 hours.
1966	IBM 7030 (Paris) computes 250,000 decimal places.
1967	CDC 6600 (Paris) computes 500,000 decimal places.
1973	Jean Guilloud and M. Bouyer in Paris compute pi to a million decimal places.
1976	Salamin and Brent find an arithmetic mean algorithm for pi.
1983	Y. Tamura and Y. Kanada compute 16 million digits in under 30 hours.
1988	Kanada computes 201, 326, 000 digits in six hours.
1989	Chudnovsky brothers find 480 million digits. Kanada calculates 536 million digits. Chudnovskys calculate 1 billion digits.
1995	Kanada computes 6 billion digits.
1996	Chudnovsky brothers compute over 8 billion digits.
1997	Kanada and Takahashi calculate 51.5 billion digits in just over 29 hours.

Decimals

16 16 7

10

Objectives
Students will:
- measure the circumference of various circular objects to the nearest millimeter.
- measure the diameter of various circular objects to the nearest millimeter.
- explain how the number pi was determined.
- demonstrate that by dividing the circumference of a circular object by its diameter you end up with pi.
- discover and demonstrate the formula for finding the circumference using pi.

NCTM Standards
- Problem solving
- Communication
- Reasoning
- Connections
- Statistics
- Measurement

Grade Level   5 - 8

Time Frame   45 minutes

Group size   pairs

Materials
✓ measuring tape
✓ string
✓ pencil
✓ assorted circular objects
✓ calculators
✓ student worksheet (pages 12 - 13)

Prerequisites
✓ Understanding of formulas
✓ Understanding of fractions and decimals

Procedure
1. Divide the class into pairs.
2. Students should find four circular objects of various sizes. Have students measure the circumference and diameters of these objects and record their findings in the chart on the student worksheet (page 13).
3. Once they have completed the measurements, they should find the ratios (circumference divided by the diameter).
4. Students should then work through the questions on the worksheet and discuss their findings.
5. You may want to give some historical information on pi at this time. Refer to the chronology and also to the student sheet on page 12.

Answers
1. answers will vary depending on objects used.
3. ratio should be approximately equal to pi.
6. $C = \pi \cdot d$

Extension
Have the whole class sit in a large circle. Someone should measure the circumference of the human circle and the diameter of the human circle. Divide the circumference by the diameter to see what value you get for pi. Discuss with the students why there is a discrepancy in the value of pi (if any). Possible answers are that the human circle is not quite a circle or difficulty in measuring the diameter of the human circle (finding the center point of the circle).

Pi — From Here to Infinity

Pi = the ratio of a circle's circumference and its diameter.

Modern computers have been used to calculate Pi to 51 billion digits.

An Egyptian scroll dating to 1650 B.C. showed Pi equal to 3.16.

Common approximations are:

$3\frac{1}{7}$ $\frac{22}{7}$

3.14   3.1416

It's irrational because it goes on and on and on.

Mathematicians have used a variety of ways to determine the value of Pi.

The exact value of Pi is a puzzle that has intrigued mathematicians for ages.

Pi is found everywhere there are round things.

Why Pi?

Name _____

Date _____

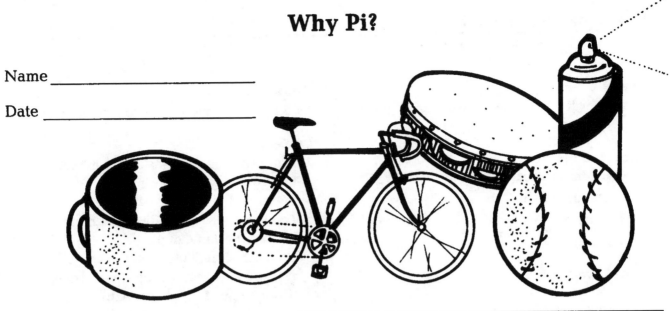

object	circumference (c)	diameter (d)	c/d (π)

1. Collect a variety of circular objects of various sizes. For each object, use a tape measure to measure the circumference and the diameter. Record the measurements in the second and third columns of the table.

2. Use a calculator to fill in the fourth column (circumference divided by diameter).

3. How does the circumference compare to the diameter?

   _____

4. This last number, the ratio of the circumference to the diameter, is called pi (π). Compare your values to 3.14. Were your calculation greater or less than the 3.14?

   _____

5. Are your values of pi consistent? Why?

   _____

6. Come up with a formula to find the circumference of a circular object knowing only the diameter of that object and the number that pi (π) represents. Demonstrate that your formula works by using it to calculate the circumference of a new circular object and then measuring the circumference to see if it is close to your calculations.

   C = _____

Objectives
Students will determine the value of pi given by Aryabhata

NCTM Standards
- Problem solving
- Communication
- Reasoning
- Connections

Grade Levels   5 - 8

Time Frame   20 minutes

Group size   Pairs

Materials
- ✓ Student worksheet (page 15)
- ✓ calculators

Prerequisite
✓ Know the area of a circle (πr^2)

Procedure
1. Introduce the students to Aryabhata (information on pages 43-47).
   Point out the location of his birth on a map. Tell students that he discovered a rule for finding the value of pi.
   On a time line, note that he lived between 476 and 550. Find his discovery in the Chronology of Pi (pages 8-10).

2. Hand out student worksheet (page 15). Have students do the calculations for question 1. Check with students to find out what values they have calculated for pi. Discuss findings as a whole group.

3. Tell them that Aryabhata had a procedure for finding the area of a circle. It was, "half the circumference multiplied by one-half the diameter." Have students complete the table.

4. Ask students to volunteer their findings. Discuss these findings as a group.

Answers
1. $\frac{62,832}{20,000} = 3.1416$

2. a. 15.708,   5,   78.54,   78.54
   b. 6.28,   2,   12.56,   12.5664
   c. 376992,   12,   452.3904,   452.3904
   Aryabhata's rule gives the correct area.

Early Computations of π

Name _____

Date _____

1. In the period between 500 to 1000 A.D., Aryabhata was one of the five mathematicians of prominence in India. His method for determining pi was this:

   "Add 4 to 100, multiply by 8, and add again 62,000. The result is approximate value of the circumference when the diameter is twenty thousand."

   Do these calculations. What value of pi does this determination yield?

   π = _____

2. Aryabhata had the following procedure for finding the area of a circle:

   "Half the circumference multiplied by half the diameter is the area of a circle."
   $(A = \frac{1}{2} C \cdot \frac{1}{2} d)$

   Do the calculations for circles with the following dimensions. Use π = 3.1416.

C	½C	d	½d	A=½C ·½d	A = πr²
31.416		10			
12.56		4			
75.3984		24			

   How accurate is Aryabhata's rule? _____

   _____

Objectives:
The student will
- extrapolate information regarding the circumference and diameter as referenced in the Bible's passage.
- show that the dimensions yield a value of 3 for pi.

NCTM Standards
- Problem solving
- Communications
- Reasoning
- Connections
- Measurement

Grade Levels   6 - 8

Time Frame   20 minutes

Group size   pairs

Materials
✓ student worksheet (page 17)
✓ calculators

Prerequisite
✓ Understanding of capacity and cubits as a unit of measure

Procedure
1. Remind students that the Bible is a religious document of both Judaism and Christianity. Note the Bible listing on the Chronology of Pi (page 8-10) at 900 B.C. Discuss how long ago that was and what life might have been like at that time. Students may need an explanation of what is meant by the notation, I Kings 7:23.

2. Hand out the student worksheet (page 17) and read the introduction. Have a student volunteer to read the passage from the Bible.

3. Review that a cubit was a unit of measure representing the distance from a man's elbow to the end of his middle finger, about 17 to 22 inches. The molten sea was a high bowl or tank supported by 12 statues of oxen, in which priests washed in preparation for religious ceremonies.

4. Have students work in pairs to answer question one. Discuss answers before moving onto questions two and three. Discuss answers to the last two questions.

Answers
1. Circumference = 30 cubits
   Diameter = 10 cubits
2. $\pi = 3$
3. 12,000 gallons

Extension
Have students find the surface area of the molten sea using the value of 3 for pi.
$$A = \pi r^2 = 3 \cdot 5 \cdot 5 = 75$$

Discuss how tall students think a bowl that is 10 cubits in diameter and holds 12,000 gallons would be and whether they think the priests needed a ladder to get to the bowl.

Pi and the Bible

Name _____

Date _____

According to the Bible, some 900 years after the Egyptians calculated pi to be about 3.1605, Solomon built a palace and a building complex. He probably used the mathematics developed by the Egyptians to aid in its construction. Part of the temple was a large bowl, called the molten sea, a high bowl or tank supported by twelve statues of oxen. Priests used it to wash their hands before religious ceremonies. The cubit was a measure of distance. It was the distance from a man's elbow to the end of his middle finger, about 17 to 22 inches. This is how the molten sea is described in the Bible.

". . . ten cubits from one brim to the other: it was round all about, and its height was five cubits: and a line of thirty cubits did compass it round about . . . It stood on twelve oxen; . . . and its brim was shaped like the brim of a cup, like a lily blossom. It contained two thousand baths."

I Kings 7: 23 - 26

1. The molten sea is described as "round all about," suggesting a circle.

What is the circumference of this circle? _____

What is the circle's diameter? _____

2. If π = C/ d, What value of π does this passage imply? Show your calculations.

π = _____

3. A bath was a liquid measure equal to approximately six gallons.
How many gallons of water could the molten sea contain? _____

Objectives
Students will
- use a geometric method of estimating pi

NCTM Standards
- Problem solving
- Reasoning
- Connections
- Patterns and functions
- Geometry
- Number relationships

Grade Levels   5 - 8

Time Frame   20 minutes

Group Size   Individual or pairs

Materials
✓ student worksheets (page 19-20)
✓ calculators
✓ compass

Prerequisite
✓ Be familiar with the formula for the area of a circle (πr^2)
✓ Able to solve simple algebraic formulas

Procedure
1. Share information with students about Srinavasa Ramanujan (pages 43-47). Explain that they will be using Srinavasa Ramanujan's geometric method for approximating pi. This is different from other methods they have studied so far.

3. As a group or in pairs have students complete the geometric method.
   - To do this, they will be constructing a quarter circle with a radius equal to $\overline{AB}$ and $\overline{AD}$. Have them visualize this as a quarter of a whole circle with a radius r.
   - They will then determine the area of the quarter circle using the formula for the area of a circle ($\frac{1}{4}\pi r^2$) and also by counting the dots within the circle.
   - They will determine the area of the square array using the formula for the area of a square (r^2) and by counting the dots (50 x 50 = 2500).
   - They will find the ratio of the circle's area to the square's area. Using the formulas from step c and d, they get ($\frac{1}{4}\pi r^2$)÷r^2 = $\frac{1}{4}\pi$. Dividing the dots they will get something close to 1960 ÷ 2500 = .785
   - They will then combine these two expressions to get a value for pi.

4. Discuss results as a whole group.

Answers
3. c) $\frac{1}{4}\pi r^2$
   d) r^2
   e) $\frac{1}{4}\pi r^2 / r^2 = \frac{1}{4}\pi$
   f) about 1960; 2500
   g) Answers will vary, but should be close to 0.785
   h) Multiply by 4. (This is because we are only considering a quarter of a circle and must multiply by 4 to get the full circle). This should give a result close to 3.14

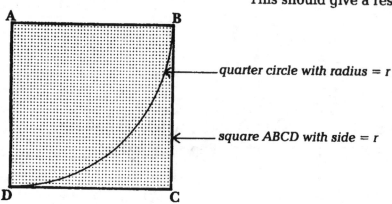

quarter circle with radius = r

square ABCD with side = r

Pin Pointing Pi

A Geometric Method Of Estimating Pi

Name _____

Date _____

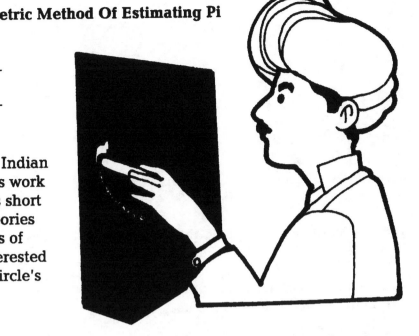

Srinavasa Ramanujan was an Indian mathematician who did most of his work during the early 1900s. During his short life he produced mathematical theories that have been used in many fields of science. One of the topics that interested Ramanujan was pi, the ratio of a circle's circumference to its diameter.

The following activity is a simple, geometric method of estimating the value of pi. It uses the 50 by 50 array of dots as shown below. Follow the instruction on page 20 to recreate his method of determining a value for pi.

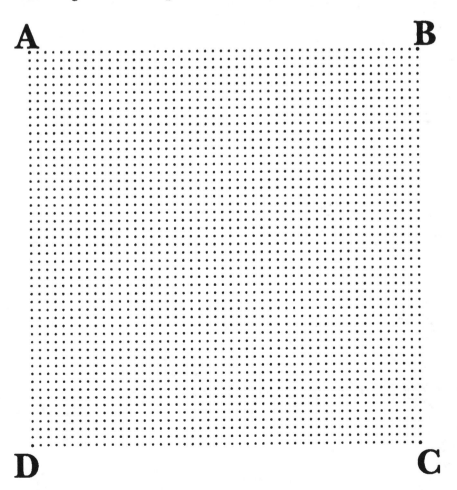

Instructions for Pin Pointing Pi

Use the 50 x 50 dot grid on page 19.

a. Place your compass point at the dot labeled A.

b. Open the compass to the dot labeled B and draw an arc from B to D.

c. Suppose the distance from A to D is r. The area of the whole circle with radius of r is πr^2.
Since you drew a quarter of this circle, the formula for the area of this quarter circle is _____ .

d. The square ABCD has sides equal to r, so the area of this square is _____ .

e. Write the ratio of the area of the quarter circle to the area of the square array.
area O / area □ = _____ (e)

f. How many dots are there in the quarter circle? _____
How many dots are in the square array? _____

g. Divide the number of dots in the quarter circle by the number of dots in the square array.
The result is _____(g).

h. What must be done with your results in part (g) to find an estimate for pi? *(Hint: refer to your answer for e).*

_____

What result does this give? π = _____

Objective

Students will
- recognize vertical lines of symmetry
- determine how groups of letters are related to pi

NCTM Standards
- Problem solving
- Reasoning
- Geometry

Grade Levels 5 - 8

Time Frame 10 minutes

Group size Individual

Materials
✓ Student worksheet (page 22)

Prerequisite
✓ Understand vertical lines of symmetry

Procedure

1. Explain that the exercise you will do in this lesson does not involve calculating the value of pi, but it shows a curious relationship between pi and the English alphabet.

2. Define which letters are vertically symmetrical. These are letters that when a line is drawn vertically through the letter it is the same on both sides of the line. The letters A, H, I, and M are vertically symmetrical.

3. Hand out student worksheet (page 22).

4. Have students begin at A and write the letters of the alphabet in capitals around the circle. Then have them cross out all the letters that are vertically symmetrical (A, H, I, M, O, T, U, V, W, X, and Y).

5. Count the remaining letters between the crossed out letters and write the number of remaining letters. Beginning with the group of numbers J-K-L, students should find that the numbers moving around the circle are 3, 1, 4, 1, 6 or when written as a decimal (3.1416) the numbers are an approximation of pi.

6. Once students discover the relation, tell them that Martin Gardner is the mathematician who pointed out this curious relationship between the symmetrical letters in an alphabet circle and pi.

Answer:
JKL - 3
N - 1
PQRS - 4
Z - 1
BCDEFG - 6
3 (.) 1 4 1 6

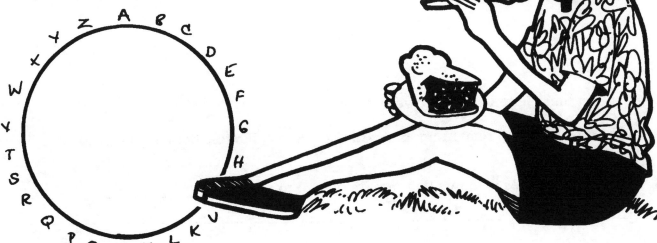

The Curious Circular π

Name _____

Date _____

1. Write the letters of the English alphabet, in capitals, clockwise around a circle.

A

2. Cross out those letters that have vertical symmetry.

3. Count the number of remaining letters in the groups of letters between the crossed out letters.

4. How are the groups of letters that remain related to π? _____

_____

Objectives

Students will:

- compare common fractions to decimals
- extend a formula for pi and compute its resulting value

NCTM Standards

- Problem solving
- Communication
- Connections
- Number and number relationships

Grade Levels 5 - 8

Time Frame   15 minutes

Group size   Pairs

Materials

✓ student worksheets (pages 24)
✓ calculators

Prerequisites

✓ Understanding of series and ability to extend a series
✓ Understanding of squaring numbers and square root

Procedure

1. Tell students that they will be calculating estimations and computations of pi done by various mathematicians. Each method yields a different number of digits beyond the decimal point as an approximation of the value for pi.

2. Hand out worksheets (page 24). Find the mathematicians on the Chronology of Pi (pages 8-10). Ask students to guess whether the calculations of the later mathematicians were more accurate than those that were completed earlier.

3. You may point out to students that Wallis's computation of pi is sometimes written as $4(\frac{2\cdot4\cdot4\cdot6\cdot6\cdot8}{3\cdot3\cdot5\cdot5\cdot7\cdot7})$ and sometimes as $2(\frac{2\cdot2\cdot4\cdot4\cdot6\cdot6\cdot8}{1\cdot3\cdot3\cdot5\cdot5\cdot7\cdot7})$. Ask them to determine if these two expressions are equivalent.

4. Have students complete the calculations.

5. Discuss answers as a whole group. In particular, determine who had the most accurate and who had the least accurate calculations.

Answers

1. a) Archimedes $\pi = 3.140845$
   b) Ptolemy $\pi = 3.141666....$
   c) Ch'ung-chih $\pi = 3.1415929292...$
   d) Bhaskara $\pi = 3.1416$
   e) Fibonacci $\pi = 3.145454545...$
   least accurate - Fibonacci
   most accurate - Ch'ung-chih

2. $\pi = 3.0021758$

Extension

Introduce students to more calculations using infinite series. Two such calculations were developed by Gottfried Leibniz and Leonhard Euler. Have students compute a value for pi using these formulas.

a) Leibniz - $\pi = 4\cdot(1 - \frac{1}{3} + \frac{1}{5} - \frac{1}{7} + \frac{1}{9} - \ldots)$

b) Euler - $\pi^2 = 6\{(\frac{1}{1})^2 + (\frac{1}{2})^2 + (\frac{1}{3})^2 + \ldots\}$

Answers

a) expanded to 10 entries - 3.041839619
b) expanded to 10 entries
   $\pi^2 = 9.298606387$
   $\pi = 3.049361636$

Getting Close to Pi

Name _____

Date _____

Most people are satisfied to know that pi is approximately 3.14. But mathematicians are funny people. They want to know **precisely** what a number is. They'll spend hours, days, even years trying to find the exact, correct answer to a problem. Throughout history many famous mathematicians have attempted to obtain accurate estimates for pi. In this lesson, you will do some calculations to find out what these famous mathematicians discovered after hours, days or years worth of work. Hopefully, it won't take you that long!

1. Use a calculator and compute how successful the following mathematicians were in their efforts. Convert their values, given here as common fractions, to decimals.

    a) **Archimedes** (240 B.C.) $\dfrac{223}{71}$ decimal _____

    b) **Claudius Ptolemy** (A.D. 150) $\dfrac{377}{120}$ decimal _____

    c) **Tsu Ch'ung-chih** (A.D. 480) $\dfrac{355}{113}$ decimal _____

    d) **Bhaskara II** (A.D. 1150) $\dfrac{3927}{1250}$ decimal _____

    e) **Fibonacci** (A.D. 1202) $\dfrac{865}{275}$ decimal _____

2. John Wallis (1616 - 1703) was a British mathematician who used an infinite product to estimate pi. An infinite series is a group of numbers that follow a pattern and that go on forever. His series began like this:

$$\pi/2 = \frac{2 \cdot 2 \cdot 4 \cdot 4 \cdot 6 \cdot 6 \cdot 8}{1 \cdot 3 \cdot 3 \cdot 5 \cdot 5 \cdot 7 \cdot 7} \quad \text{or} \quad \pi = 2 \cdot \left\{ \frac{2 \cdot 2 \cdot 4 \cdot 4 \cdot 6 \cdot 6 \cdot 8}{1 \cdot 3 \cdot 3 \cdot 5 \cdot 5 \cdot 7 \cdot 7} \right\}$$

Extend the expression to 10 entries in both the numerator and denominator. Then, using a calculator, compute the resulting value of pi.

$$\pi = \text{_____}$$

Objectives

Students will

- measure the circumferences of their heads
- demonstrate that when you measure the circumference of a head, then divide by pi, your get your hat size

NCTM Standards:

- Problem solving
- Communications
- Reasoning
- Connections
- Measurement

Grade Levels 5 - 8

Time Frame   15 minutes

Group size   Pairs or groups of three

Materials

- ✓ student worksheet
- ✓ calculators
- ✓ various hats with the sizes shown
- ✓ flexible measuring tape

Prerequisite

- ✓ Be familiar with circumference and able to measure the circumference of circles

Procedure

1. Explain to students that they will be discovering another strange phenomena related to the number pi. This lesson involves the relationship between pi and the size of their heads.

2. Divide students into groups.

3. Give each group of students the worksheet and a measuring tape (inches).

4. Walk them through the directions on the student sheet. Have them use the tape to measure the circumferences of their heads and record the numbers in the second column of the chart. Give them the value of 3.1416 to use for pi (third column). Have them divide the circumferences by pi and record the results in the fourth column.

5. Then have each person try on hats until he or she finds a hat that fits. The hat size should be noted in the last column.

6. When they have recorded the data, they should check to see if indeed they have found their hat size; that is, if the numbers in the last two columns are approximately equal. Ask students what would they need to do to their results to get a more accurate hat sizes.

Answers

Answers will vary. Round off their results to the nearest one-eighth inch.

Hats Off to Pi

Names

Names _____

_____

_____

Date _____

For this lesson you will demonstrate how you can find your hat size using pi. Use this table to record your answers.

name	circumference	π	C/π	hat size

1. Measure the circumference of the head of each person in your group and record the measurements in the second column of the table.

2. Divide the circumference by π and record the quotient in the fourth column.

3. Try on several hats to find a hat that fits. Record the hat's size in the last column.

4. Does your hat size match your calculation of C/π ? _____

   If not, what do you need to do to your calculation to get a more accurate result?

   _____

   _____

   _____

Objective

Students will discover why it is said that "pi are squared," or how pi relates to various squared numbers.

NCTM Standards
- Problem solving
- Numbers and number theory
- Communications

Grade Levels   5 - 8

Time Frame   10 minutes

Group size   Individual or pairs

Materials
- ✓ student worksheet (page 28)
- ✓ calculator

Prerequisite
- ✓ Understanding of squaring numbers and square roots

Procedure

1. Review squaring numbers.

2. Explain to students that in this lesson they will explore the Greek number system and see how pi (as well as the letters p and i) have a unique relationship in the Greek number system and with other numerals. Explain that in the Greek system, letters stood for numbers, and so the symbol Π (capital p) was used to denote the number 80. Review the Greek number system. Explain that ancient Greeks used the 24 letters of the Greek alphabet plus three

obsolete letters to denote numbers. The first nine letters represented numbers one through nine. The next nine letters represented numbers ten to ninety. The last nine letters represented multiples of one hundred. At first capital letters were used. Later they used lower case letters.

3. Hand out the student sheets (page 28).

4. Have the students work through the activity. You may wish to do the first question together, so they see how to count the letters and fill in the blanks. Remind them not to count obsolete numbers. In the first question they would fill in the blanks so it reads, π is the _16th_ letter and _16_ is the square of _4_.

5. As a whole class discuss if anyone has any other insights into other patterns.

Answers

1. 16, 16, 4
2. 16, 9, 3
3. 16, 9, 25, 5
4. 16, 9, 144, 12
5. 16, 4, 4, 2

Extension

Teach students how to write numbers using the Greek system, which is an additive system.
Example:
NB = 50 + 2 = 52
ΨΙΗ = 700 + 10 + 8 = 718
ΧΘ = 600 + 9 = 609
ΣΝΔ = 200 + 50 + 4 = 254

Squaring Off with Pi

Name _____

Date _____

The symbol for pi comes from the Greek alphabet, a system that was used both for writing words and numbers. The symbol Π is the capital letter p and the symbol π is the lower case letter p. This is the Greek number system.

A	*alpha*	1	I	*iota*	10	P	*rho*	100
B	*beta*	2	K	*kappa*	20	Σ	*sigma*	200
Γ	*gamma*	3	Λ	*lambda*	30	T	*tau*	300
Δ	*delta*	4	M	*mu*	40	Y	*upsilon*	400
E	*epsilon*	5	N	*nu*	50	Φ	*phi*	500
obsolete		6	Ξ	*xi*	60	X	*chi*	600
Z	*zeta*	7	O	*omicron*	70	Ψ	*psi*	700
H	*eta*	8	Π	*pi*	80	Ω	*omega*	800
Θ	*theta*	9	obsolete		90	obsolete		900

This activity will show you one of the many fascinating discoveries that can be made from the constant pi. By answering the questions you will find out how pi relates to squared numbers.

Note: When you are counting the letters, do not count obsolete letters.

1. In the Greek alphabet, Π is the (a) _____th letter, and (a) _____ is the square of (b) _____.

2. In the English alphabet, *p* is also the (a) _____th letter. The letter *i* is the (c) _____ th letter, which is the square of (d) _____.

3. Add (a) _____ and (c) _____ and you get (e) _____, which is the square of (f) _____.

4. Multiply (a) _____ and (c) _____ and you get (g) _____, which is the square of (h) _____.

5. Divide (a) _____ by (b) _____, and you get (b) _____, the square of (i) _____.

Objectives

Students will

- perform an experiment to determine an approximation for pi
- discover that the probability is directly related to the value of pi

NCTM Standards:

- Problem solving
- Communication
- Reasoning
- Connections
- Probability

Grade Levels   6 - 8

Time Frame   40 minutes

Group size   Groups of three or four

Materials

- ✓ toothpicks or straws
- ✓ large sheets of white paper
- ✓ calculators
- ✓ student worksheet (page 30)

Prerequisite

- ✓ Knowledge of probability
- ✓ Solving literal equations

Procedure

1. Review some basic probability concepts. Then tell students that they will perform a famous experiment what was devised in the late 1700s to estimate the value of pi using probability. Comte de Buffon, a French mathematician, originated this experiment. Find his entry on the Chronology of Pi and information about his life on pages 43- 47.

2. Divide students into groups of three or four. Give the groups all the materials they will need for the experiment.

3. Read the brief introduction to the experiment.

4. Walk the students through the procedures of the experiment.

5. When groups have obtained their estimates for pi, have them share their results with the class.

Answers

To obtain better results you can play around with the experimental arrangements (how many lines to use, how high up the toothpicks should be when it is dropped, etc.). The more tosses, the closer the result is to the value of pi. Also, choosing d just a little bigger than L works best.

When solving for P you get

$$P = i/n \text{ and } P = 2L/\pi d$$
$$\text{since } i/n = 2L/\pi d$$
$$\text{then } \pi di/n = 2L$$
$$\text{or } \pi id = 2Ln$$
$$\text{and } \pi = (2Ln)/(id)$$

Using their values for i, n, L, and d, they can calculate π.

The explanation of why the formula $P = 2L/\pi d$ works is not easy to give since it involves calculus. The explanation can, however, be found in Peter Beckman's book, *A History of Pi*.

Extensions

Have groups compare their results. Ask them to think about what they could do to ensure better results (a closer value to pi). Discuss the fact that they would have to perform this experiment a large number of times. The best results from this experiment were by an Italian mathematician in 1901. He made 3408 tosses and found π correct to six decimal places.

The π Needle Experiment

Name _____

Date _____

One of the most interesting and unusual methods for estimating π was discovered by the French mathematician Georges Louis Leclerc, Comte de Buffon, who wrote:

Let a needle of length L be thrown at random onto a horizontal plane ruled with parallel straight lines spaced by a distance d (greater than L) from each other. What is the probability that the needle will intersect one of these lines?

He calculated that the probability (P) that the needle will fall across one of these lines was P = 2L/πd (where P is the number of intersects of the needle divided by number of drops).

Follow these directions to perform a similar experiment.

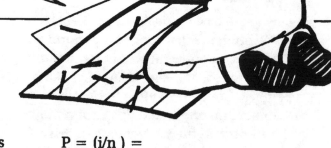

> **a.** Take a large sheet of white paper and tape it to the floor.
>
> **b.** Carefully draw parallel lines (one direction only). The distance (d) between the lines should be a little larger than the length (L) of the toothpicks that you are using.
>
> **c.** Standing next to the paper, randomly drop the toothpicks from different locations around the paper.
>
> **d.** Keep track of the number of times you dropped the toothpick (n) and the number of times the toothpick intersects one of the lines (i).

1. Calculate the experimental probability.

total number of intersects (i) = _____

total number of drops (n) = _____

probability = total intersects ÷ total drops   P = (i/n) = _____

2. Using the results from your experiment and the formula P = 2L/πd, find an approximation for pi. *(Hint: Replace P with i/n and solve the literal equation for π.)*

Objectives

Students will use an the binary search method to determine the approximate value for the square root of pi.

NCTM Standards

- Numbers and number theory
- Connections

Grade Levels 5 - 12

Time Frame 15 - 20 minutes

Group size Individual or pairs

Materials

✓ student worksheet
✓ calculator

Prerequisites

- Understand how to square numbers and find square root on a calculator
- Able to compare decimals, smallest to largest
- Able to find the average of two numbers

Procedure

1. Review square root. Once students understand the concept and can find the square root of common numbers like 9, 49, 144, etc., have them find the square roots of several numbers using their calculators.

2. Tell students that mathematicians wondered if it was possible to find the square root of pi. Because pi is irrational, it cannot have a rational square root, but what mathematicians were looking for was a number that was close to a square root. With this activity, they will go through the same steps and find a value that is close to the square root of pi.

3. Hand out the student work sheet (page 32). Go through the following example as a whole class:

- Choose $S = \underline{1}$ and $L = \underline{2}$.
- $S^2 = \underline{1}$ and $L^2 = \underline{4}$.
- Since S^2 is farther away from pi than L^2, S gets replaced with the average of S and L (which is $\underline{1.50}$).
- Now $S^2 = \underline{2.25}$ and $L^2 = \underline{4}$.
- Since S^2 is farther away from pi than L^2, S gets replaced with the average of S and L (which is $\underline{1.75}$).
- Now $S^2 = \underline{3.0625}$ and $L^2 = \underline{4}$.
- L^2 is farther away from pi, so L gets replaced with the average of S and L (which is $\underline{1.875}$).
- Now $S^2 = \underline{3.0625}$ and $L^2 = \underline{3.515625}$.
- Since L^2 is farther away from pi, L gets replaced with the average of S and L (which is $\underline{1.8125}$).
- Now $S^2 = \underline{3.0625}$ and $L^2 = \underline{3.28515625}$.
- Again L^2 is farther away from pi, so L gets replaced with the average of S and L ($\underline{1.781250}$)
- So, we have $S = \underline{1.75}$ and $L = \underline{1.78125}$
- At this point we know that the square root of pi lies between $\underline{1.75}$ and $\underline{1.78125}$. If we continue this process we can get finer and finer bounds for the value of the square root of pi. After a while we will see that the square root of pi equals $\underline{1.77245}$. . . Since pi is irrational we can never get an exact answer. We have to settle for an approximation.

4. Have students follow the directions as outlined using new numbers.

5. Walk around and assist students who are confused.

Extension

Can the binary method be used to find the square root of any number? Try it on several numbers.

Closing In on the Square Root of Pi

Name _____

Date _____

You know that $\sqrt{9} = 3$ and $\sqrt{100} = 10$, but what about the square root of an irrational number like π? For a long time mathematicians wondered, "If pi is irrational, is it possible to find its square root?" There is a method called the **binary search method** that will find the square root of pi, or at least a close approximation to the square root.

1. Pick a value you know to be too small to be the square root of pi. Call this S (for small value).

2. Pick a value you know to be too large to be the square root of pi. Call this L (for large value).

3. Find S^2 and L^2.

4. Which of these values (S^2 or L^2) is farther away from pi?
   If S^2 is farther away than L^2, then replace S with the average of S and L, otherwise replace L with the average of S and L.

5. Repeat the process with new values for S, L, S^2 and L^2.

6. As before, compare the value to see which is farther away from pi. Replace the one that is farther away from pi with the average of S and L.

7. Continue this process until you get a lower and upper bound for the square root of pi.

S = _____   L = _____

S^2 = _____ L^2 = _____

_____ is farther from pi.

Find average of S and L
$\dfrac{S+L}{2} =$ _____

Replace _____ with the average.

S = _____   L = _____

S^2 = _____ L^2 = _____

_____ is farther from pi.

Find average of S and L
$\dfrac{S+L}{2} =$ _____

Replace _____ with the average.

S = _____   L = _____

S^2 = _____ L^2 = _____

Continue on the back of this paper.

Objective
Students will estimate the value of pi by plotting points taken from a random sample.

NCTM Standards
- Problem solving
- Connections
- Reasoning
- Statistics
- Communications

Grade Levels 7 - 8

Time Frame   20 - 25 minutes

Group Size   Groups of three or four

Materials
- ✓ graph paper
- ✓ calculators
- ✓ telephone books
- ✓ student worksheets (page 34-35)
- ✓ compass

Prerequisites
- ✓ Knowledge of plotting coordinates
- ✓ Understand the concept of random numbers
- ✓ Understanding of ≤ and ≥ symbols

Pairs of random numbers will be in this quadrant.

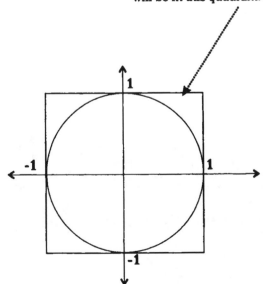

Procedures
1. Divide students in groups of three or four.

2. Have students select two phone numbers and make decimals using the last four numbers.
   - ◆ Explain what a unit circle is (whose equation is $x^2 + y^2 = 1$).
   - ◆ Using a compass with a radius 1, have students draw a unit circle with center at (0, 0).
   - ◆ Students should then make a square so that the circle is inscribed into a square.

3. Then have students plot the coordinate point that was generated by the phone numbers.

4. Steps 1 through 6 in the student directions should be repeated so that they have a large sample of numbers. These also should be plotted on the graph.

5. They now should count all the points that are in the quarter circle.
   Combining the formulas for probability
   $P = k/n$ and $P = \pi/4$
   they get $\pi/4 = k/n$
   or $\pi = 4(k/n)$

6. As a whole class discuss question ten.

Answers
9. a) $\pi r^2 = \pi$, since r = 1
    b) $(2r)^2 = 4r^2 = 4$, since r = 1
    d) $\pi r^2/ 4r^2$ $= \pi/4$
    e) $\pi = 4 \cdot prob(x^2 + y^2) < 1)$
    g) $4k/n$

10. The number of points in the unit circle and the distribution of random numbers

Extension
Try the experiment with several more numbers. Explain why you think that the ratio $4k/n$ should be approximately equal to pi.

Randomly Looking for Pi

Name _____

Date _____

Who would guess that you can find π between the covers of a phone book? People have devised many ways of finding π. One way that you can easily do this involves using random numbers, and one way to generate random numbers is to use telephone numbers that are randomly selected from a telephone book.

Plotting the Points

1. **Pick numbers** - Look through a telephone book and pick any telephone number.

2. **Make a decimal** - Using only the last four digits, insert a decimal point in front of the four-digit number. For example, if you picked the number 563-7867, you would select the last four digits (7867) and place a decimal point in front of it, making .7867. Call this number x.

3. **Choose another number** - Choose another telephone number, retaining only the last four digits, and repeat the same procedure. Call this number y.

4. **Make an ordered pair** - The two numbers you have chosen, x and y, will become the coordinate point (x, y) on a graph.

5. **Construct a graph** - On a piece of graph paper, draw a unit circle (with equation $x^2 + y^2 = 1$) circumscribed into a square as shown in the diagram to the right.

   The side of the square is 2 units and the radius of the circle is 1. You will only be using the first quadrant of the circle.

6. **Plot point** - Plot the point (x, y). This point will be in the square, but not necessarily in the circle.

7. **Repeat** - Repeat this procedure several times with other pairs of telephone numbers (n pairs). For each pair, plot the corresponding point (x, y).

Calculating Pi

8. **Count pairs** - Count the number of pairs for which the distance $r \leq 1$; that is, pairs that are inside the circle. Call this number k.

$k =$ _____

Count that total number of coordinate points (those graphed inside and outside the circle) and call this n.

$n =$ _____

9. **Question** - Now if you pick a random point (x, y), what is the probability that this random point lies inside the unit circle (i.e., $P(x^2 + y^2 < 1)$?

    a) area of circle = _____

    b) area of square = _____

    c) given that Prob $(x^2 + y^2 < 1)$ = area of circle ÷ area of square

    d) then Prob$(x^2 + y^2 < 1)$ = _____

    e) using the equation in (d), $\pi =$ _____

    f) combine (d) with Prob$(x^2 + y^2 < 1)$ = total number of points in a circle (k) divided by the total number of points (n)

    g) then $\pi =$ (approximately) _____

10. **Question** - On what does the accuracy of pi depend?_____

Objective
The student will use Archimedes' "classical" method to determine bounds for the value of pi

NCTM Standards
- Problem solving
- Reasoning
- Connections
- Geometry

Grade Levels   7 - 8

Time Frame   15 - 20 minutes

Group size   Individual or pairs

Materials
- ✓ straightedge
- ✓ compass
- ✓ calculator
- ✓ protractor
- ✓ student worksheet

Prerequisites
- ✓ Ability to construct a hexagon
- ✓ Familiarity with basic concepts in geometry
- ✓ Ability to calculate perimeters of polygons
- ✓ Understand the meaning of tangency

Procedure
1. Introduce students to Archimedes by sharing information found on pages 43-47. Find his entry on the Chronology of Pi (pages 8-10). Explain that Archimedes was very interested in the number π, and he succeeded in coming closer to its value than any of the other mathematicians in ancient Egypt or Babylonia.

   While this "classic" method is one of the oldest and it is easy to understand the basic concept, the calculations can be challenging. It is advisable to walk students through the proof.

2. Demonstrate the basic concept by showing students a circle that has a diameter of 1 unit length and an equilateral triangle inscribed in it. Make another equilateral triangle circumscribed about the circle. The circumference of the circle is less that the perimeter of the large triangle but greater than the perimeter of the small triangle. Since C = π·d and d = 1, C = π. Therefore, perimeter small Δ < π < perimeter large Δ. By using polygons with ever-increasing numbers of sides, it is possible to move closer and closer to the value of π. Tell students that they will use this method with a hexagon.

3. Divide students in pairs and hand out the student worksheets (page 38-39).

4. *(steps 1-3)* To determine the perimeter of an inscribed regular hexagon, students should construct the radii of the circle to each of the two adjacent vertices of the hexagon, forming an equilateral triangle with one side of the hexagon (see diagram). Students should be able to determine the side of the hexagon is equal to the radius (because the triangle is an equilateral triangle) and, thus, the perimeter of the hexagon is equal to 6r.

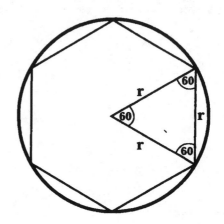

5. *(step 4)* Given that the circumference of the circle is greater than the perimeter of the inscribed hexagon, students should be able to write an inequity, using pi, that states this fact. They should write:

$2\pi r > 6r$

Solving the equation for π, they get

$\pi > 6r/2r$

$\pi > 3$

<u>Highlight this answer as it will be needed later.</u>

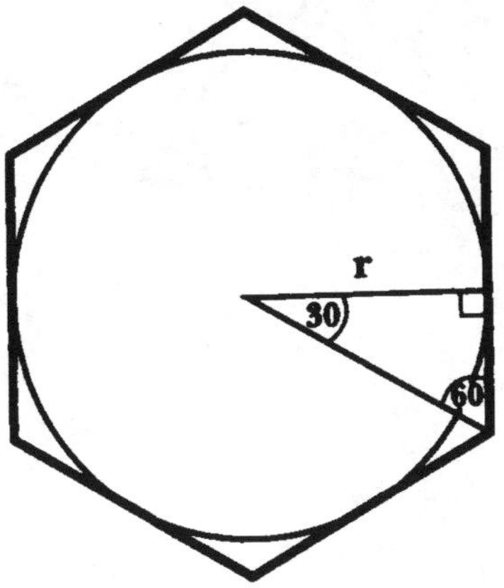

6. *(step 5)* Now, to determine the perimeter of the circumscribed hexagon, they should first start by constructing a circumscribed hexagon and then construct a segment from the center of the circle to one of vertices of the hexagon and a radius to the point of tangency of a side terminating at that vertex (see diagram above).

7. *(step 6)* Ask students what kind of triangle these two segments together with half a side of the hexagon form (30-60-90 degree triangle). Since the ratio of the sides of a 30-60-90 triangle is always $1 - \sqrt{3} - 2$ (so the formula $a^2 + b^2 = c^2$ is true), this information can be used to find the relative lengths of the triangle's sides. While this information is given in instructions for step 6, go through why this is so. The side of the triangle that is the radius of the circle (r) is equal to $\sqrt{3} \cdot h$ or $h = r/\sqrt{3}$.

8. *(step 7)* Given that h is one half a side of the hexagon, students should determine the perimeter of the hexagon; $p = 12\,h$

They then need to express the perimeter in terms of r by substituting the value of h they determined in step six ($r/\sqrt{3}$). See the answers for number 7 below for the results.

9. *(step 8)* Have them write an inequality, using pi, stating that the circumference of the circle is less than the perimeter of the hexagon. Students should then solve for pi.

10. *(step 9)* Now have students combine their two inequalities ($\pi > 3$ and $\pi < 3.4641.\ .\ .$) to find the upper and lower bounds for pi.

11. Tell students that Archimedes' method was unsurpassed for 19 centuries. In 1610, Ludolph van Ceulen (Dutch, 1540 - 1610) computed an approximation for pi to 35 decimal places using polygons having 2^{62} sides. With the emergence of calculus and analytic geometry at the beginning of the eighteenth century, better methods for determining pi's value were developed.

Answers

3. radius; $p_{hexagon} = 6r$

4. $2\pi r > 6r$; $\pi > 3$

6. $r = \sqrt{3}\,h$ and $h = r/\sqrt{3}$

7. $p = 6(2h) = 12 \cdot h$

$p = 12(r/\sqrt{3}\,)$

$p = 12(\dfrac{r}{\sqrt{3}} \cdot \dfrac{\sqrt{3}}{\sqrt{3}})$

$p = 12\,(\dfrac{r \cdot \sqrt{3}}{3})$

$p = 4\sqrt{3}r$

8. $2\pi r < 4\sqrt{3}r$; $\pi < 2\sqrt{3} = 3.4641$

9. Between 3 and about 3.4641

Extension

Discuss the fact that the results are not very precise, but they may be improved by increasing the number of sides of the polygon. As the number of sides increases, the bounds move closer together, and the value of pi can more nearly be determined.

The Pi Phenomenon

Name _____

Date _____

It is believed that the first scientific attempt to compute π was made by Archimedes in about 240 B.C. He used what is called the "classical method" using circles and polygons. With this activity, you will determine the upper and lower bounds of pi using regular hexagons that are inscribed in and circumscribed around a circle.

Draw an Inscribed Hexagon

1. Using a compass, draw a circle and construct a regular hexagon inside the circle.

2. Draw the radii (r) of the circle to each of the two adjacent vertices of the hexagon, forming an equilateral triangle with one side of the hexagon.

3. Each side of the hexagon has the same length as the _____ of the circle, so the perimeter of the hexagon is _____.

4. The circumference of the circle (2πr) is greater than the perimeter of the inscribed hexagon. Write an inequality stating this fact and then solve for π.

_____ > _____

π > _____

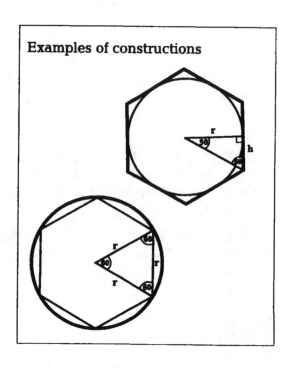

Examples of constructions

Draw a Circumscribed Hexagon

5. Draw a circumscribed
   hexagon. To determine the
   circumscribed hexagon's
   perimeter, construct a
   segment from the center of
   the circle to one of the
   vertices of the hexagon and
   the radius to the point of
   tangency of a side
   terminating at that vertex.

6. In the triangle, if r is the
   side of the triangle formed
   by the radius, and h is the
   shortest side, $r = \sqrt{3} \cdot h$.
   Solve this formula for h.

   $h =$ _____

7. If h is one half a side of the hexagon, what is the perimeter of the
   hexagon (written in terms of h)?

   $P_{hexagon} =$ _____

   Substitute the value for h (from step 6) to get a formula for the
   perimeter expressed in terms of r.

   $P_{hexagon} =$ _____
   $\phantom{P_{hexagon}} =$ _____

8. The circumference of the inscribed circle is less than the perimeter of the hexagon.
   Write an inequality stating this fact and then solve for π.

   _____

   _____

   $\pi <$ _____

9. Now combing the two inequalities (the one from step 4 and the one from step 8),
   what two values does π lie between?

   _____ $< \pi <$ _____

Where Do You Find Pi?

Where do you find pi? Anywhere you find a circle. Since pi is a ratio between a circle's circumference and diameter, it is used to find the value for area and volume of two and three-dimensional figures that have circular shapes. Here are some common formulas that use the number pi.

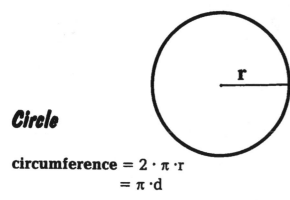

Circle

circumference = $2 \cdot \pi \cdot r$
$\qquad\qquad\quad = \pi \cdot d$

area = $\pi \cdot r^2$

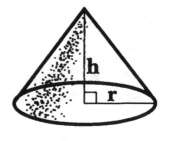

Sphere

volume = $\frac{4}{3} \cdot \pi \cdot r^3$

surface area = $4 \cdot \pi \cdot r^2$

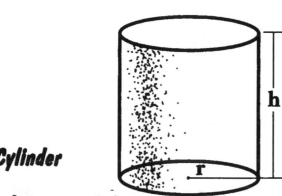

Cylinder

volume = $\pi \cdot r^2 \cdot h$

surface area = $2 \cdot \pi \cdot r^2 + 2 \cdot \pi \cdot r \cdot h$
$\qquad\qquad\quad = 2 \cdot \pi \cdot r^2 + h)$

Cone

volume = $\frac{1}{3} \cdot \pi \cdot r^2 \cdot h$

40

Remembering Pi

Mnemonics is a way of remembering something by assigning words to the letters or numbers. People have developed ways to remember value of pi by writing poems and sentences. Here are a few examples. Count the number of letters in each word to see if the phrase gives a value for pi.

For I know I chose knowledge to attain life's goal.
3 . 1 4 1 5   9   2 6 5 4

*Hey, I want a fully memorable pi poetry
Which has newly arranged sentences.*

_____

*See, I have a rhyme,
Assisting my feeble brain,
Its tasks ofttimes resisting.*

_____

Write your own sentences to help you remember the value for pi.

_____

_____

_____

_____

Glossary

area - The measurable surface contained within any plane geometrical figure, usually measured in square units (square feet, square inches, square centimeters, square meters).

circumference - the perimeter of a circle, the value of which is $2\pi r$.

cubit - An ancient linear unit based on the length of the forearm, usually between 17 and 21 inches.

coordinate pair - A pair of numbers that indicate placement of the coordinate point on a graph. If (x, y) is the coordinate pair, x determines horizontal distance and y determines vertical distance, both measured from the graph's central point, (0, 0).

decimal - a fraction that has as its denominator a power of ten. Fractions like $\frac{7}{10}$ and $\frac{27}{100}$ are written as .7 and .27 and are terminating decimals. Repeating decimals are of the form .33333. . . Decimals that are neither terminating or repeating are irrational numbers.

diameter - a straight line segment that passes through the center of a circle and joins two opposite points on the circle. Its length is equal to two radii.

equilateral - all sides of the given figure have the same measure.

hexagon - a closed straight-line polygon having six sides. If all sides are equal, it is a regular hexagon.

irrational number - A number that cannot be expressed exactly as a ratio of two integers. The decimal expression of these numbers in neither terminal or repeating.

perimeter - The outer boundary of a two-dimensional figure. The sum of the sides of the figure.

pi - The ratio of the circumference of a circle to its diameter. It is an irrational number, but its approximate value is 3.14159+. A more elementary approximation is $3\frac{1}{7}$.

polygon - A plane closed broken-line figure. A regular polygon has equal angles and equal sides.

probability - The relative frequency with which an event occurs or is likely to occur.

random numbers - Numbers that are selected in such a way that each number has an equal probability of being chosen.

ratio - The quotient of two numbers, most usually written as a fraction.

rational number - A number that can be expressed as a fraction, where both the numerator and denominator are integers.

square - To multiply a number by itself.

square root - A number which when multiplied by itself yields the given number. For example, the square root of 16 ($\sqrt{16}$) is +4 or -4.

symmetrical - Having the characteristic that it is the same size, form and arrangement on one side of a point or line as on the opposite side.

tangent - touching at a single point

Information About the Mathematicians

Archimedes (c. 287 - 212 BC)

This resident of Syracuse was born about 287 B.C. on the island of Sicily. He studied at the great Museum in Alexandria. In his work he explained many of the principles of basic physics. Perhaps the most famous incident involving Archimedes' scientific talents was the "bath episode" in which his principle was used to test the gold in the crown and it was found to be a fake.

Archimedes also developed a "classical" method for determining the bounds for the value of pi. This method was based on the idea that the circumference of a circle must lie between the perimeters of its inscribed and circumscribed polygons. When these perimeters have been determined, they give upper and lower bounds for the circumference of the circle and, thus, the value of pi. Using a 96-sided polygon, Archimedes determined that the value of π was between $223/71$ and $22/7$. Using this method, Ptolemy 400 years later used a polygon of 360 sides to determine a value of pi equal to 3.1416. In 1596 Ludolph of Cologne used this method to calculate pi to 32 decimal places. This number was engraved on his tombstone and Germans still call pi the Ludolphine number.

Aryabhata (476 - 550)

Aryabhata was born (A.D.476) at Kasumapura, the City of Flowers, a small town in India. His work consists of a collection of astronomical tables and a treatise on arithmetic. Other work shows a knowledge of the quadratic equation and of the indeterminate linear equation.

Aryabhata was twenty-three years of age when he wrote *Aryabhatiya*, which he finished in 499. This contains an introduction of 10 verses, followed by a section on mathematics with 33 verses, then a section of 25 verses on the reckoning of time and planetary models, with the final section of 50 verses being on the spheres and eclipses.

Georges Leclerc, Comte de Buffon (1707 - 1788)

Buffon's father, Benjamin Leclerc, was a state official in Burgundy; his mother was a woman of spirit and learning, and he was fond of saying that he got his intelligence from her. The name Buffon came from an estate that he inherited from his mother.

At the age of 20, Georges Buffon discovered the binomial theorem. He corresponded with Cramer on mechanics, geometry, probability, number theory, and differential and integral calculus.

He is remembered most in mathematics for a probability experiment that he carried out, calculating pi by throwing sticks over his shoulder onto a tiled floor and counting the number of times the sticks fell across the lines between the tiles. This experiment caused much discussion among mathematicians and helped towards an understanding of probability.

Buffon also had a lasting influence in some areas of natural science. He was the first to reconstruct geological history in a series of stages. With his notion of lost species, he opened the way to the development of paleontology. He was the first to propose the theory that the planets had been created in a collision between the sun and a comet. His *Histoire Naturelle* was the first work to present the previously-isolated and apparently disconnected facts of natural history in a generally intelligible form.

Bhaskara II (1114 - 1185)

Bhaskara was an Indian mathematician born in Biddar, India. He was also known as "Bhaskara the Learned." He was the leading mathematician of the twelfth century. His first works were on the systemic use of the decimal number system. He developed rules for equations to calculate trigonometry and used letters to represent unknown quantities, as in modern algebra, several centuries before any similar developments in Europe. He understood zero and negative numbers and studied Pell's equation, finding several solutions. Bhaskara was also an astronomer. He popularized the astronomical knowledge of his time and headed the astronomical observatory at Ujjain, India.

Bhaskara rightly achieved an outstanding reputation for his contributions. In 1207 an educational institution was set up to study his works.

Ludolph Van Ceulen (1540 - 1610)

Ludolph was born in Germany in 1540. He spent most of his life approximating 35 decimal places of pi using polygons of size 2^{62}. It was fitting that at his death his tombstone was engraved with the number 3.14159265358979323846264338327950288, since it really was the point and purpose of his life. It is amazing that a scientist with such dedication to the discovery of knowledge does not have much written about him.

Leonhard Euler (1707 - 1783)

Leonhard Euler was a Swiss mathematician born in Basel on April 15, 1707. His father was an accomplished mathematician and a Calvinist minister. He trained his son in elementary mathematics and also to follow in his role as a pastor of the village church. Euler, however, developed a love for mathematics and chose to follow a mathematical career.

He spent most of his life teaching in Russia and Germany. In 1727 he was invited to teach mathematics at the new St Petersburg Academy.

Early in his career, Euler suffered from severe health problems and almost lost his life. By the age of 50 he was blinded due to cataracts. On September 18, 1783, Euler died of a stroke.

Euler wrote on topics ranging from artillery and sound to lotteries, navigation, and magnetism. He is credited with revising almost all branches of mathematics. Modern mathematics owes a great debt to Euler. He was the first to use the small letters a, b, and c to indicate the sides of a triangle and the corresponding upper case A, B, and C for the opposite angles. He standardized the use of the letter e to represent the base of the system of natural logarithms. His work established the use of the Greek letter π for the ratio of the circumference to the diameter in a circle.

One of the greatest problems Euler was attributed with solving was the legendary "Bridges of Konisberg" problem. Euler used networks, vertices and arcs to describe the problem, and the problem eventually gave birth to the fascinating mathematical study of topology.

Leonardo Pisano Fibonacci (1170 - 1250)

Fibonacci was born in Pisa, Italy but was educated in North Africa where his father held a diplomatic post. He traveled widely with his father, recognizing the enormous advantages of the mathematical systems used in the countries they visited.

Fibonacci ended his travels around the year 1200 and returned to Pisa. There he wrote a number of important texts that played an important role in reviving ancient mathematical skills and made significant contributions of his own. One of the books he published was titled *Liber Abaci* (*Book of Counting*). This book introduced the Hindu-Arabic numerals and their competing schemes to the European audience. Before this, most arithmetic calculations were still done on an abacus and recorded in Roman

44

numerals. Fibonacci introduced a new system. The Fibonacci sequence was also introduced at this time.

Fibonacci also wrote an applied geometry book that included work on surveying, methods for finding square and cube roots, and some considerations in algebra and geometry. Fibonacci was the greatest European mathematician of his time.

James Gregory (1638 - 1675)

James Gregory was born in Durmoak (near Aberdeen), Scotland. James learned mathematics first from his mother, who taught geometry, and later his brother took over his education. He was given Euclid's *Elements* to study, which he found quite easy.

Gregory attended Maiscal College in Aberdeen where he began to study optics and the construction of telescopes. In 1664 Gregory went to Italy, where he spent most of his time at the University of Padua. There he worked on using infinite convergent series to find areas of circles and hyperbolas. He also worked to prove that π and e are transcendental. He went to Edinburgh in 1674 and became the first person to hold the Chair of Mathematics.

One night he was showing the moons of Jupiter to his students with telescopes when he suffered a stroke and became blind. He died a few days later at the young age of 36. His remarkable contributions include:

- discovering the Taylor expansions more than 40 years before Taylor
- solving Kepler's famous problem of how to divide a semicircle by a straight line through a given point of the diameter in a given ratio
- defining the integral
- first to prove that π and e are not the solution of algebraic equations
- expressing the sum of the nth powers of the roots of an algebraic equation in terms of the coefficients.

Gottfried Wilhelm von Leibniz
(1646 - 1716)

Gottfried Wilhelm Leibniz was the son of a German university professor who died when Gottfried was only six years old. By the time Leibniz was eight years old, he had learned Latin; by twelve he knew Greek. Much of his knowledge was obtained through self-study by reading the books in his family's library. At fifteen he entered the university, embarking on a study of law. Since his interests were very broad, he also undertook studies in mathematics, philosophy and theology. He eventually obtained a law degree and began work as a diplomat, an occupation that he pursued for the rest of his life.

In 1672 a diplomatic mission brought Leibniz to Paris, which at the time was the intellectual center of the Western world. There he studied mathematics and physics under Christian Huygens. Between 1672 and 1676 Leibniz developed his principles for calculus. He continually sought a universal mathematics-like language that could be used to obtain solutions for any scientific problem. This eventually lead to formulating a system of deductive logic. Leibniz is responsible for the decimal point system and writing numerical exponents. He was also the first person to introduce the term "function" into mathematical language

Leibniz was also a very religious man and was fascinated by religions and cultures of the East. He devised a theory whereby God was represented by the number one, and the void by zero; and by combining these two numbers in binary arithmetic, demonstrated how creation took place.

Leibniz led an extremely productive and varied life. When he died in 1716 only his secretary attended his funeral.

Sir Isaac Newton (1643 - 1727)

Isaac Newton was the son an English farming family of modest means. Though he experimented with many small devices, exhibiting a talent for inventing, he did not do well in school.

Newton's life changed when he entered Trinity College in Cambridge. He studied for a law degree but soon began to read books by mathematicians such as Kepler, Euclid and Descartes. This eventually lead to his interest in mathematics. He abandoned his studies in law and embarked on serious studies and experimentation in mathematics, physics, astronomy, theology, and alchemy.

When the bubonic plague hit England in 1665, the university was closed for two years. Newton returned to his country home and immersed himself in mathematical studies. During this time he devised his method of differential calculus. Upon returning to Cambridge, Newton worked in optics, discovered the composition of white light, and developed a theory of light based on a concept of particles.

In 1669, Newton became a professor of mathematics at Trinity College where he continued his work and befriended astronomer Edmund Halley. By 1685 Newton completed his major work, the *Principia*. In this book he introduced a theory of gravitation that explained why the planets travel in elliptical orbits and, in so doing, completed the scientific picture Kepler had drawn of the solar system.

The *Principia* also contained the three principal laws of motion. These laws would revolutionize the study of dynamics. His work was praised through Europe; however, he was still embroiled in controversy. The French upheld Descartes' theory of vortices against Newton's principles of gravity. Gottfried Wilhelm Leibniz released his own theory of the calculus, starting the dispute as to who invented calculus first. This controversy plagued Newton for the rest of his life.

In 1696, Newton became master of the British mint and remained a highly respected scientist. In 1705 he was honored by being made a knight of the British Empire for his contributions to British science.

Srinavasa Ramanujan (1887-1920)

Srinavasa was born in southern India in the town of Kumbakonam. He was primarily self-educated and developed a fascination for the study of mathematics. He was quiet and possessed an exceptional memory. He would entertain his friends by reciting lists of Sanskrit roots as well as mathematical values for pi and the square root of 2 to many decimal places.

At age 16 he began college, aided by a government scholarship; however, within a year he lost his scholarship due to his lack of proficiency in English. At the urging of his friends, Ramanujan wrote to England's foremost mathematicians, describing over one hundred theorems from various branches of mathematics.

G.H. Harding, of Trinity College, Cambridge, England, was overwhelmed by what he read in the correspondence. Harding recognized that this was the work of an amazing mathematical talent and wrote, "I have never seen anything like them before. . . They must be true because, if they were not, no one would have had the imagination to invent them." Thus began an extraordinary five-year collaboration of the two men who had little in common except a love of mathematics.

During his five-year collaboration with Harding, Ramanujan published more than thirty papers on various mathematical topics. His theories eventually influenced cancer research and pyrometry (the study of very high temperatures).

In 1917 Ramanujan fell ill and returned to India. Despite his illness, he remained sharp and his interest in mathematics keen. Once while visiting Ramanujan's sickbed, Harding said that he had arrived in a taxi that bore the

46

dull number 1729. The bedridden patient responded that no, the number was really interesting, as it could be represented as the sum of two cubes in two different ways, $9^3 + 10^3$ and $12^3 + 1^3$.

Ramanujan died in 1920 at the age of 32. Fortunately his wife kept track of the sheets of paper he filled with mathematical formulas, which came to be known as the "Lost Notebook." More than 70 years after his death, his work is still an important source of new mathematical ideas. One of his series formulas has been used in computer computations to calculate millions of digits in the decimal expansion of pi. Modern physicists have used Ramanujan's partition discoveries to solve problems in statistical mechanics.

Tsu Ch'ung Chih (430 - 501)

Tsu was a Chinese mathematician and astronomer. He gave the rational approximation 355/113 to pi that is correct to 6 decimal places. He also proved that pi is between 3.1415926 and 3.1415927. While it would be nice to know more about this remarkable result, his book, written with his son, is lost.

Tsu's astronomical achievements include the making of a new calender in 463 that never came into use. He also determined the precise time of the solstice by measuring the length of the sun's shadow at noon on days near the solstice to reduce errors caused by the fact that it is very difficult to determine the exact time of the solstice.

John Wallis (1610 - 1703)

John Wallis first became interested in mathematics when he attended Emmanuel College in Cambridge in 1630. Since nobody at Cambridge at this time could direct his mathematical studies, his main topic of study became divinity. He was ordained in 1640.

Wallis was skilled in cryptography and decoded Royalist messages for the Parliamentarians during the Civil War. He was part of a group interested in natural and experimental science who started to meet in London. This group was to become the Royal Society, so Wallis was a founding member of the Royal Society and one of its first Fellows.

Wallis contributed substantially to the origins of calculus and was the most influential English mathematician before Newton. He devised a method of interpolation and, using Kepler's concept of continuity, he discovered methods to evaluate integrals. He introduced our present day symbol for infinity.

Wallis was responsible for restoring some ancient Greek texts of Ptolemy and Arisarchus. Some of his non-mathematical works include many religious works, and books on etymology, grammar and logic.

Resources For Pi

Beckman, Petr. *A History of* π. New York: St Martin's Press, 1976.

Lennart Berggren, Peter Borwein and Jonathan Borwein. *Pi: A Source Book*. New York: Springer-Verlag, 2000.

Apostol, Tom. *The Story of Pi*. (Computer-animated videotape.) Washington, DC: National Council of Teachers of Mathematics, 1989.

Zerger, Monte. "The Magic of Pi." *Journal of Recreational Mathematics* 12 (1979): 21-23.

Eves, Howard. "The Latest About Pi." *Mathematics Teacher* 55 (February 1962): 129-30.